YOUR WORD

HAS GIVEN ME LIFE

MEDITATIONS ON

CHRISTIAN VIRTUES

MICHAEL HABASHI

St. Athanasius St. Cyril Theological School (ACTS) Press

1617 W. La Palma Ave, Anaheim, CA 92801

www.acts.press

Special discounts are available on quantity purchases by corporations, associations, and others. For details, contact ACTS Press.

Printed in the United States of America

ISBN: 978-1-940661-88-9

DEDICATION

To my father SAINT BASIL THE GREAT,
   who guides me with his heart

To my father SAINT AUGUSTINE OF HIPPO,
   who inspires me with his tears

To my father HIS HOLINESS POPE SHENOUDA III,
   who teaches me with his eyes

TABLE OF CONTENTS

AUTHOR'S NOTE

I am humbled that you have selected this book. This has been a lengthy and challenging labor of love.

This work began in earnest in February 2019 when I started serious self-study of the church fathers; in parallel, I decided to capture key Bible passages related to the fruit of the Spirit – all for my own edification and growth in my spiritual journey. As I read more, I began to dig deeper into the fruit of the Spirit and the many other virtues embodied in our Lord and Savior Jesus Christ.

This book contains meditations on twenty-five of those virtues, which I find sum up the life of the true Christian. Their application to the atheist, agnostic, or believer of a different faith is also highly defensible; the words speak for themselves.

Each chapter is dedicated to a virtue and you will find three sources of inspiration within:

1. An opening poem I wrote for your meditation and prayer

2. A quotation from an Orthodox Church father on the virtue; I have included a mix of ancient and modern fathers from both the Oriental and Eastern families

3. Selections from the Bible (NKJV translation) on the virtue

In gathering passages and writing about these virtues, I felt an inexplicable amount of God's grace. There were small signs here and there. For example, while completing my draft of this book on an extended retreat at Saint Paul Coptic Orthodox Abbey in Murrieta, California, I kept returning to the chapter on faithfulness. I had selected an opening quotation from Saint Augustine of Hippo that I was not completely satisfied with, as it spoke about *faith* as opposed to *faithfulness*. I knew I had to reference Saint Augustine somewhere in the text, but this saying of his was not quite what I needed. I scoured my personal database of sayings of the church fathers and could not find anything by him that really spoke to the virtue. I then *had* the idea of going back to my notes on his *Confessions*. I typed "faithfulness" in the search bar and, lo and behold, the perfect words appeared:

We were overwhelmed by our sins; we had fallen away from You into the depths of darkness, and Your good Spirit was moving over us, ready to bring help when the time was due. You made just men of sinners and set them apart from the wicked; You established the authority of Your Book between those above, who would be obedient to You, and those beneath, who would be made subject to them; and You gathered all the faithless together into one body, so that the earnest devotion of the faithful might be clearly seen and they might bear You fruit in works of mercy, by distributing their worldly wealth to the poor in order to acquire heavenly riches for themselves. You willed that the faithful, by providing them with what they need for temporal use, should do good works that would bear fruit in the future life.

The title of this book is a tribute to one of my favorite Bible verses: Psalm 119:50. Within this book are nearly four hundred meditations; to that end, you may use this book for daily reflection, and let God's Word give life, meaning, and purpose to your days and years. You might also pick up this book when you desire comfort, advice, or wisdom – during the heights of joy and depths of tribulation. Regardless of the occasion of your reading, I hope you will always find this work beneficial for your life of virtue and meditation.

I am forever indebted to His Grace Bishop Kyrillos for his love and support and for making this publication possible. Special thanks also to my editor Dena Beshai and all the staff at ACTS Press.

Finally, thank you for joining me on this journey of meditation. I invite you to discover the hidden treasures along the way, immersing your mind, heart, and soul within these pages and sharing them with the world around you that you might be the city set on the hill.

m.

December 2020

INTRODUCTION

O we no one anything except to love one another, for he who loves another has fulfilled the law. For the commandments, "You shall not commit adultery," "You shall not murder," "You shall not steal," "You shall not bear false witness," "You shall not covet," and if *there* is any other commandment, are *all* summed up in this saying, namely, "You shall love your neighbor as yourself." Love does no harm to a neighbor; therefore love *is* the fulfillment of the law.

> And *do* this, knowing the time, that now *it is* high time to awake out of sleep; for now our salvation is nearer than when we *first* believed. The night is far spent, the day is at hand.
>
> Therefore let us cast off the works of darkness, and let us put on the armor of light. Let us walk properly, as in the day, not in revelry and drunkenness, not in lewdness and lust, not in strifeand envy. But put on the Lord Jesus Christ, and make no provision for the flesh, to fulfill its lusts. (Romans 13:8-14)

I have long been consumed by this commandment of the Apostle Paul to "put on the Lord Jesus Christ".

Pope Shenouda III, the 117th Pope of the Coptic Orthodox Church and one of my greatest inspirations, once said that there are certain verses in the Bible that are like hard candies – ones whose sweetness we keep in our mouth and hope never dissolve. "Put on the Lord Jesus Christ" (Romans 13:14) is one of those delicious verses. It sounds so simple, but within it we can find the whole of Christianity.

If we think about what it means to put something on – a shirt, skirt, jacket – it covers our skin, it covers our nakedness.

It is important to look back at the first mention of clothing in the Bible:

> So when the woman saw that the tree *was* good for food, that it *was* pleasant to the eyes, and a tree desirable to make *one* wise, she took of its fruit and ate. She also gave to her husband with her, and he ate. Then the eyes of both of them were opened, and they knew that they were naked; and they sewed fig leaves together and made themselves coverings.
>
> And they heard the sound of the Lord God walking in the garden in the cool of the day, and Adam and his wife hid themselves from the presence of the Lord God among the trees of the garden.
>
> Then the Lord God called to Adam and said to him, "Where are you?"
>
> So he said, "I heard Your voice in the garden, and I was afraid because I was naked; and I hid myself." (Genesis 3:6-10)

The fig leaves had a two-fold purpose for Adam and Eve: to cover their sin and to hide their fear.

When Saint Paul instructs us to "put on the Lord Jesus Christ," he is telling us that Christ is our garment.

Saint Ephrem the Syrian writes, "Our Savior came and underwent suffering in order to heal Adam's wounds and provide a garment of glory for his nakedness." (*Commentary on the Diatessaron*)

Christ is our garment of fig leaves. Even in sin and fear, we are called to put on Christ. Just as the clothing we wear protects us from the cold and hides the imperfections, cuts, bruises, and scars on our bodies – putting on Christ envelops us with the warmth of Christ, the True

Physician.

But what does it mean to actually put on Christ? Can anyone put on Christ? Have you ever put on a shirt or sweater and the tag in the back bothered you? Is there anything wrong with the shirt, or sweater, or the tag? No. It is our skin responding to the tag.

Imagine Christ as the sweater – to put on Christ and not be itchy; we have to accept the sweater – with its tag. We have to change. To that end, we have to make our bodies prepared and holy.

So how do we put on Christ?

We put on Christ when we love and live the life of virtue.

Saint Basil the Great writes, "May God grant that we through virtue may become like Him." (*Letter V*)

In Matthew 3:8 and Luke 3:8, Christ instructs us to "bear fruits worthy of repentance". These fruits – the outputs and signs of our repentance and regret – essentially acts of faith and love, are the requirements of the life of virtue.

As our spirituality matures, we advance to bear the fruit of the Spirit. These are the powers and possessions of the mind and heart – the characteristics or qualities of Christ – that all men should acquire through our work and the grace of God:

"But the fruit of the Spirit is love, joy, peace, longsuffering, kindness, goodness, faithfulness, gentleness, self-control." (Galatians 5:22-23)

If we truly love and respect the Lord, we must try to be like Him in all ways. We must learn from Him. We must learn of His love, His joy, His peace, His longsuffering, His kindness, His goodness, His faithfulness, His gentleness, His self-control.

This book is a meditation on those nine virtues – and many more.

Saint John Chrysostom writes:

> There is a great distance between virtue and evil, and a great difference. One is wide and easy, but the other is

narrow and full of tribulation. Luxury is wide and easy,
but poverty and need are narrow and full of tribulation.
So just as in this life the ways are opposed – the person
who chooses virginity travels the narrow road of tribulation, and so does the person who pursues chastity,
embraces voluntary poverty, and scorns vainglory; but
the person who is eager to travel on the wide and easy
road surrenders himself to drunkenness, luxury, madness
for money, licentiousness, and harmful spectacles – the
difference between them is great; so also in the time of
punishment and recompense, there is a great distance to
be found between their requitals. (*On Wealth and Poverty*)

This book is meant to lead you down the path of self-examination – to
contemplate that vast distance and that great difference between virtue
and evil.

In another passage of *On Wealth and Poverty*, Saint John Chrysostom
urges us:

In order not to be chastised hereafter, in order not to
undergo punishment hereafter, let each of us enter into
his own conscience, unfold the story of his life, examine
all his transgressions accurately, condemn his soul which
has committed such acts, correct his intentions, afflict
and straighten his thoughts. Let him seek a penalty for
his sins by self-condemnation, by complete repentance,
by tears, by confession, by fasting and almsgiving, by
self-control and charity, so that in every way we may become able to put aside all our sin in this life to depart to
the next life with full confidence. (*On Wealth and Poverty*)

Around fifteen centuries later, Saint Habib Girgis, a recently canon-
ized Coptic saint and revolutionary educator, proclaimed Chrysostom's
same spirit of self-reflection for our salvation:

Each one of us needs to place in front of him a statue
of the characteristics of such men who struggled for the

truth and defended it with a death-defying defense, and to make our lofty goal to be to walk a walk worthy of our kinship to Christ. We ask God to plant in us the love of virtue and to remove from our hearts the thorns of sin, in order for us to bear fruit worthy of repentance - and He is capable of rescuing us from the pit that we are in, for He is capable of all things. (*A Religious Lecture on the Christian Religion*)

With this book in your hands, you are equipped with the opportunity to meditate on the life of virtue with the support of the sayings of the church fathers, the Holy Bible, and the words of my weakness. You may find your thoughts ascending to the mountain – where all your senses may experience the virtues of our Lord and Savior Jesus Christ, where all your thoughts may be consumed with love for Him.

May God grant us – through the grace of His Holy Spirit – life, healing, inspiration, and guidance through these words.

ON FAITH

My soul seeks everlasting life
My satisfaction comes from You
Unite me with Your will
Flood me with rivers of living water
Bless my land with summer fruits
Prune my branches of fear and doubt
Grant O Lord that I may be FAITH

✳ ✳ ✳ ✳ ✳

Planning based on knowledge is tiresome, but faith is everything. The Lord is the only one who manages all our matters. Be still and the Lord will fight for you. Let us have patience with those who return evil for good. God rewards everyone according to his deeds. Taking action or being still are in God's hand. A foot does not move ahead of the other without His permission. Lay your burdens upon the Lord, and He will take care of you.

KYRILLOS VI OF ALEXANDRIA

SCHOOL OF VIRTUE

✳ ✳ ✳

✝ Therefore I say to you, do not worry about your life, what you will eat or what you will drink; nor about your body, what you will put on. Is not life more than food and the body more than clothing? Look at the birds of the air, for they neither sow nor reap nor gather into barns; yet your heavenly Father feeds them. Are you not of more value than they? Which of you by worrying can add one cubit to his stature? So why do you worry about clothing? Consider the lilies of the field, how they grow: they neither toil nor spin; and yet I say to you that even Solomon in all his glory was not arrayed like one of these. Now if God so clothes the grass of the field, which today is, and tomorrow is thrown into the oven, *will* He not much more *clothe* you, O you of little faith? Therefore do not worry, saying, "What shall we eat?" or "What shall we drink?" or "What shall we wear?" For after all these things the Gentiles seek. For your heavenly Father knows that you need all these things. But seek first the kingdom of God and His righteousness, and all these things shall be added to you. (MATTHEW 6:25-33)

✝ For by grace you have been saved through faith, and that not of yourselves; *it is* the gift of God, not of works, lest anyone should boast. (EPHESIANS 2:8-9)

✝ Trust in the Lord with all your heart,
And lean not on your own understanding;
In all your ways acknowledge Him,
And He shall direct your paths.
(PROVERBS 3:5-6)

✝ For we walk by faith, not by sight. (2 CORINTHIANS 5:7)

✝ The genuineness of your faith, being much more precious than gold that perishes, though it is tested by fire, may be found to praise, honor, and glory at the revelation of Jesus Christ, whom having not seen you love. (1 PETER 1:7-8)

✝ Let us draw near with a true heart in full assurance of faith, having our hearts sprinkled from an evil conscience and our bodies washed with pure water. (HEBREWS 10:22)

✝ Though now you do not see *Him*, yet believing, you rejoice with joy inexpressible and full of glory, receiving the end of your faith—the salvation of your souls. (1 PETER 1:8-9)

✝ Now faith is the substance of things hoped for, the evidence of things not seen. (HEBREWS 11:1)

✝ But without faith *it is* impossible to please *Him*, for he who comes to God must believe that He is, and *that* He is a rewarder of those who diligently seek Him. (HEBREWS 11:6)

✝ Preserve me, O God, for in You I put my trust. *O my soul,* you have said to the Lord, "You are my Lord, My goodness is nothing apart from You." (PSALM 16:1-2)

✝ Have faith in God. For assuredly, I say to you, whoever says to this mountain, "Be removed and be cast into the sea," and does not doubt in his heart, but believes that those things he says will be done, he will have whatever he says. Therefore I say to you, whatever things you ask when you pray, believe that you receive *them*, and you will have *them*. (MARK 11:22-24)

✝ If you confess with your mouth the Lord Jesus and believe in your heart that God has raised Him from the dead, you will be saved. For with the heart one believes unto righteousness, and with the mouth confession is made unto salvation. (ROMANS 10:9-10)

✝ Pursue righteousness, godliness, faith, love, patience, gentleness. Fight the good fight of faith, lay hold on eternal life (1 TIMOTHY 6:11-12).

✝ For as the body without the spirit is dead, so faith without works is dead also. (JAMES 2:26)

✝ The purpose of the commandment is love *from* a pure heart, *from* a good conscience, and from sincere faith. (1 TIMOTHY 1:5)

✝ Therefore, having been justified by faith, we have peace with God through our Lord Jesus Christ, through whom also we have access by faith into this grace in which we stand, and rejoice in hope of the glory of God. And not only *that*, but we also glory in tribulations, knowing that tribulation produces perseverance; and perseverance, character; and character, hope. (ROMANS 5:1-4)

✝ Count it all joy when you fall into various trials, knowing that the testing of your faith produces patience. (JAMES 1:2-3)

✝ *As for* God, His way *is* perfect;
The word of the Lord *is* proven;
He *is* a shield to all who trust in Him.
(2 SAMUEL 22:31)

✝ In God I have put my trust;
I will not be afraid. (PSALM 55:11)

✝ For with God nothing will be impossible. (LUKE 1:37)

ON WORKS

My hands raise in thanksgiving
My reins seek to please You
Shepherd me with Your rod and staff
Ground me in Your will
Anoint my actions with love
Let my light shine that all may see
Grant O Lord that I may be WORKS

✳ ✳ ✳ ✳ ✳

Let us hasten with all energy and readiness of mind to perform every good work. For the Creator and Lord of all Himself rejoices in His works. For by His infinitely great power He established the heavens, and by His incomprehensible wisdom He adorned them. With His holy and undefiled hands He formed man, the most excellent, and truly great through the understanding given him — the express likeness of His own image. He approved them, and blessed them, and said, "Increase and multiply." We see, then, how all righteous men have been adorned with good works, and how the Lord Himself, adorning Himself with His works, rejoiced. Having therefore such an example, let us without delay accede to His will, and let us work the work of righteousness with our whole strength.

CLEMENT OF ROME

EPISTLE TO THE CORINTHIANS

✳ ✳ ✳

✝ Let your light so shine before men, that they may see your good works and glorify your Father in heaven. (MATTHEW 5:16)

✝ For we are His workmanship, created in Christ Jesus for good works, which God prepared beforehand that we should walk in them. (EPHESIANS 2:10)

✝ What *does it* profit, my brethren, if someone says he has faith but does not have works? Can faith save him? If a brother or sister is naked and destitute of daily food, and one of you says to them, "Depart in peace, be warmed and filled," but you do not give them the things which are needed for the body, what *does it* profit? Thus also faith by itself, if it does not have works, is dead. (JAMES 2:14-17)

✝ Do not forget to do good and to share, for with such sacrifices God is well pleased. (HEBREWS 13:16)

✝ And whatever you do, do it heartily, as to the Lord and not to men, knowing that from the Lord you will receive the reward of the inheritance; for you serve the Lord Christ. (COLOSSIANS 3:23-24)

✝ Let us not grow weary while doing good, for in due season we shall reap if we do not lose heart. (GALATIANS 6:9)

✝ Be steadfast, immovable, always abounding in the work of the Lord, knowing that your labor is not in vain in the Lord. (1 CORINTHIANS 15:58)

✝ Command those who are rich in this present age not to be haughty, nor to trust in uncertain riches but in the living God, who gives us richly all things to enjoy. *Let them* do good, that they be rich in good works, ready to give, willing to share, storing up for themselves a good foundation for the time to come, that they may lay hold on eternal life. (1 TIMOTHY

6:17-19)

✝   For as the body without the spirit is dead, so faith without works is dead also. (JAMES 2:26)

✝   Trust in the Lord, and do good;
Dwell in the land, and feed on His faithfulness.
Delight yourself also in the Lord,
And He shall give you the desires of your heart.
(PSALM 37:3-4)

✝   It is God who works in you both to will and to do for *His* good pleasure. (PHILIPPIANS 2:13)

✝   Who *is* wise and understanding among you? Let him show by good conduct *that* his works are *done* in the meekness of wisdom. (JAMES 3:13)

✝   We know that all things work together for good to those who love God, to those who are the called according to *His* purpose. (ROMANS 8:28)

✝   Learn to do good;
Seek justice,
Rebuke the oppressor;
Defend the fatherless,
Plead for the widow. (ISAIAH 1:17)

ON PRAYER

My groaning resounds eastward
My soul yearns for You
Hear me when I cry
Pull me into Your warm embrace
Let my breath draw us closer
Lift my chin and comfort me
Grant O Lord that I may be PRAYER

✶ ✶ ✶ ✶ ✶

Prayer is the experience of being in God's presence. Prayer is an effective power that brings us into contact with the Christ who is actually present within us. In prayer, God's personal will and ours meet. Prayer that is spiritual and genuine is both a call and a response: a divine call and a human response.

MATTHEW THE POOR

ORTHODOX PRAYER LIFE

❋ ❋ ❋

✝ I cried out to the Lord because of my affliction,
And He answered me.
Out of the belly of Sheol I cried,
And You heard my voice.
For You cast me into the deep,
Into the heart of the seas,
And the floods surrounded me;
All Your billows and Your waves passed over me.
Then I said, "I have been cast out of Your sight;
Yet I will look again toward Your holy temple."
The waters surrounded me, even to my soul;
The deep closed around me;
Weeds were wrapped around my head.
I went down to the moorings of the mountains;
The earth with its bars closed behind me forever;
Yet You have brought up my life from the pit,
O Lord, my God.
When my soul fainted within me,
I remembered the Lord;
And my prayer went up to You,
Into Your holy temple. (JONAH 2:2-7)

✝ Seek the Lord while He may be found,
Call upon Him while He is near. (ISAIAH 55:6)

✝ The Lord is near to all who call upon Him,
To all who call upon Him in truth.
He will fulfill the desire of those who fear Him;
He also will hear their cry and save them. (PSALM 145:18-19)

✝ You, O Lord, are a shield for me,
My glory and the One who lifts up my head.
I cried to the Lord with my voice,
And He heard me from His holy hill. (PSALM 3:3-4)

✝ If My people who are called by My name will humble

themselves, and pray and seek My face, and turn from their wicked ways, then I will hear from heaven, and will forgive their sin and heal their land. (2 CHRONICLES 7:14)

✝ Give ear to my prayer, O God,
And do not hide Yourself from my supplication.
Attend to me, and hear me;
I am restless in my complaint, and moan noisily. (PSALM 55:1-2)

✝ Rejoice always, pray without ceasing, in everything give thanks; for this is the will of God in Christ Jesus for you. (1 THESSALONIANS 5:16-18)

✝ Now this is the confidence that we have in Him, that if we ask anything according to His will, He hears us. And if we know that He hears us, whatever we ask, we know that we have the petitions that we have asked of Him. (1 JOHN 5:14-15)

✝ Watch and pray, lest you enter into temptation. The spirit indeed is willing, but the flesh is weak. (MATTHEW 26:41)

✝ Continue earnestly in prayer, being vigilant in it with thanksgiving. (COLOSSIANS 4:2)

✝ How long, O Lord? Will You forget me forever?
How long will You hide Your face from me?
How long shall I take counsel in my soul,
Having sorrow in my heart daily?
How long will my enemy be exalted over me?
Consider and hear me, O Lord my God;
Enlighten my eyes. (PSALM 13:1-3)

✝ Be anxious for nothing, but in everything by prayer and supplication, with thanksgiving, let your requests be made known to God; and the peace of God, which surpasses all understanding, will guard your hearts and minds through Christ Jesus. (PHILIPPIANS 4:6-7)

✝ Hear me when I call, O God of my righteousness!
You have relieved me in my distress;
Have mercy on me, and hear my prayer.
(PSALM 4:1)

✝ Is anyone among you suffering? Let him pray. Is anyone cheerful? Let him sing psalms. Is anyone among you sick? Let him call for the elders of the church, and let them pray over him, anointing him with oil in the name of the Lord. And the prayer of faith will save the sick, and the Lord will raise him up. And if he has committed sins, he will be forgiven. Confess your trespasses to one another, and pray for one another, that you may be healed. The effective, fervent prayer of a righteous man avails much. Elijah was a man with a nature like ours, and he prayed earnestly that it would not rain; and it did not rain on the land for three years and six months. And he prayed again, and the heaven gave rain, and the earth produced its fruit. (JAMES 5:13-18)

✝ Assuredly, I say to you, if you have faith and do not doubt, you will not only do what was done to the fig tree, but also if you say to this mountain, "Be removed and be cast into the sea," it will be done. And whatever things you ask in prayer, believing, you will receive. (MATTHEW 21:21-22)

✝ Give ear to my words, O Lord,
Consider my meditation.
Give heed to the voice of my cry,
My King and my God,
For to You I will pray.
My voice You shall hear in the morning, O Lord;
In the morning I will direct it to You,
And I will look up. (PSALM 5:1-3)

✝   I spread out my hands to You;
My soul longs for You like a thirsty land. Selah
Answer me speedily, O Lord;
My spirit fails!
Do not hide Your face from me,
Lest I be like those who go down into the pit.
Cause me to hear Your lovingkindness in the morning,
For in You do I trust;
Cause me to know the way in which I should walk,
For I lift up my soul to You. (PSALM 143:6-8)

ON HUMILITY

My eyes glimpsed my wretchedness
My vessel now emptied for You
Engulf me with Your Spirit
Hold me as the little child
Manage my life as You deem fit
Satisfy my soul as with marrow and fatness
Grant O Lord that I may be HUMILITY

✻ ✻ ✻ ✻ ✻

True humility does not say humble words, nor does it assume humble looks, it does not force oneself either to think humbly of oneself, or to abuse oneself in self-belittlement. Although all such things are the beginning, the manifestations and the various aspects of humility, humility itself is grace, given from above. There are two kinds of humility, as the holy fathers teach: to deem oneself the lowest of all beings and to ascribe to God all one's good actions. The first is the beginning, the second the end.

GREGORY OF SINAI

ON COMMANDMENTS AND DOGMA

✳   ✳   ✳

✝ Then Jesus called a little child to Him, set him in the midst of them, and said, "Assuredly, I say to you, unless you are converted and become as little children, you will by no means enter the kingdom of heaven. Therefore whoever humbles himself as this little child is the greatest in the kingdom of heaven. Whoever receives one little child like this in My name receives Me." (MATTHEW 18:2-5)

✝ Humble yourselves in the sight of the Lord, and He will lift you up. (JAMES 4:10)

✝ All of *you* be submissive to one another, and be clothed with humility, for "God resists the proud, But gives grace to the humble." Therefore humble yourselves under the mighty hand of God, that He may exalt you in due time, casting all your care upon Him, for He cares for you. (1 PETER 5:5-6)

✝ If anyone desires to come after Me, let him deny himself, and take up his cross daily, and follow Me. (LUKE 9:23)

✝ Walk worthy of the calling with which you were called, with all lowliness and gentleness, with longsuffering, bearing with one another in love. (EPHESIANS 4:1-2)

✝ He has shown you, O man, what *is* good;
And what does the Lord require of you
But to do justly,
To love mercy,
And to walk humbly with your God? (MICAH 6:8)

✝ The fear of the Lord *is* the instruction of wisdom,
And before honor is humility. (PROVERBS 15:33)

✝ By humility *and* the fear of the Lord
Are riches and honor and life. (PROVERBS 22:4)

✝   Let nothing *be done* through selfish ambition or conceit, but in lowliness of mind let each esteem others better than himself. Let each of you look out not only for his own interests, but also for the interests of others. Let this mind be in you which was also in Christ Jesus, who, being in the form of God, did not consider it robbery to be equal with God, but made Himself of no reputation, taking the form of a bondservant, and coming in the likeness of men. And being found in appearance as a man, He humbled Himself and became obedient to the point *of* death, even the death of the cross. (PHILIPPIANS 2:3-8)

✝   Do not set your mind on high things, but associate with the humble. (ROMANS 12:15)

✝   Whoever exalts himself will be humbled, and he who humbles himself will be exalted. (LUKE 14:11)

ON REPENTANCE

My tears exceed the sand of the sea
My soul mourns the sins of my past
Wash me with the dew of Your mercy
Restore me to Your salvation
Wipe my eyes with the wool of Gideon
Accept my brokenness as a sacrifice
Grant O Lord that I may be REPENTANCE

*   *   *   *   *

Repentance is not despondency but eager expectation; it is not to feel that one has reached an impasse, but to take the way out. It is not self-hatred but the affirmation of my true self as made in God's image. To repent is to look, not downward at my own shortcomings, but upward at God's love; not backward with self-reproach, but forward with trustfulness. It is to see, not what I have failed to be, but what by the grace of Christ I can yet become.

KALLISTOS OF DIOKLEIA

THE INNER KINGDOM

✳ ✳ ✳

✝ The Lord your God is gracious and merciful, and will not turn His face from you if you return to Him. (2 CHRONICLES 30:9)

✝ Have mercy upon me, O God,
According to Your lovingkindness;
According to the multitude of Your tender mercies,
Blot out my transgressions. (PSALM 51:1)

✝ Bear fruits worthy of repentance. (MATTHEW 3:8)

✝ The Lord is not slack concerning His promise, as some count slackness, but is longsuffering toward us, not willing that any should perish but that all should come to repentance. (2 PETER 3:9)

✝ I have not come to call the righteous, but sinners, to repentance. (LUKE 5:32)

✝ If we confess our sins, He is faithful and just to forgive us our sins and to cleanse us from all unrighteousness. (1 JOHN 1:9)

✝ As many as I love, I rebuke and chasten. Therefore be zealous and repent. Behold, I stand at the door and knock. If anyone hears My voice and opens the door, I will come in to him and dine with him, and he with Me. (REVELATION 3:19-20)

✝ Turn to Me with all your heart,
With fasting, with weeping, and with mourning. (JOEL 2:12)

✝ Return to Me, and I will return to you. (ZECHARIAH 1:3)

✝ The Lord is near to those who have a broken heart,
And saves such as have a contrite spirit. (PSALM 34:18)

✝ The sacrifices of God are a broken spirit,

A broken and a contrite heart—
These, O God, You will not despise. (PSALM 51:17)

✝   I say to you that likewise there will be more joy in heaven over
one sinner who repents than over ninety-nine just persons who
need no repentance. (LUKE 15:7)

✝   I will give them a heart to know Me, that I am the Lord; and
they shall be My people, and I will be their God, for they shall
return to Me with their whole heart. (JEREMIAH 24:7)

ON GRACE

My flesh longs for You
My depths desire Your favor
Decorate me with the wings of the eagle
Fly me to the heights of Your glory
Let my eyes find You
Shower my countenance with Your splendor
Grant O Lord that I may be GRACE

✸ ✸ ✸ ✸ ✸

We do not see Christ externally, we meet Him within us. Christ takes shape in us. The faithful become Christ's by grace. What happens is a miraculous interpenetration by grace and an identification without confusion. The whole man, in body and in spirit, enters the unalloyed world of the uncreated grace of the Trinity. And at the same time he receives into himself Christ, with the Father and the Holy Spirit.

VASILEIOS OF STAVRONIKITA

HYMN OF ENTRY

✳   ✳   ✳

✝ To each one of us grace was given according to the measure of Christ's gift. (EPHESIANS 4:7)

✝ As each one has received a gift, minister it to one another, as good stewards of the manifold grace of God. (1 PETER 4:10)

✝ But now the righteousness of God apart from the law is revealed, being witnessed by the Law and the Prophets, even the righteousness of God, through faith in Jesus Christ, to all and on all who believe. For there is no difference; for all have sinned and fall short of the glory of God, being justified freely by His grace through the redemption that is in Christ Jesus. (ROMANS 3:21-24)

✝ For by grace you have been saved through faith, and that not of yourselves; it is the gift of God, not of works, lest anyone should boast. For we are His workmanship, created in Christ Jesus for good works, which God prepared beforehand that we should walk in them. (EPHESIANS 2:8-10)

✝ Let us therefore come boldly to the throne of grace, that we may obtain mercy and find grace to help in time of need. (HEBREWS 4:16)

✝ The law was given through Moses, but grace and truth came through Jesus Christ. (JOHN 1:17)

✝ If I have found grace in Your sight, show me now Your way, that I may know You and that I may find grace in Your sight. (EXODUS 33:13)

✝ And lest I should be exalted above measure by the abundance of the revelations, a thorn in the flesh was given to me, a messenger of Satan to buffet me, lest I be exalted above measure. Concerning this thing I pleaded with the Lord three times that it might depart from me. And He said to me, "My grace is sufficient for you, for My strength is made perfect in weakness." (2 CORINTHIANS 12:7-9)

✝   He who loves purity of heart
     And has grace on his lips,
     The king will be his friend. (PROVERBS 22:11)

✝   You, O Lord, are a God full of compassion, and gracious,
     Longsuffering and abundant in mercy and truth. (PSALM
     86:15)

✝   The Lord God is a sun and shield;
     The Lord will give grace and glory;
     No good thing will He withhold
     From those who walk uprightly. (PSALM 84:11)

✝   Unto the upright there arises light in the darkness;
     He is gracious, and full of compassion, and righteous.
     A good man deals graciously and lends;
     He will guide his affairs with discretion. (PSALM 112:3-5)

✝   You open Your hand
     And satisfy the desire of every living thing.
     The Lord is righteous in all His ways,
     Gracious in all His works.
     The Lord is near to all who call upon Him,
     To all who call upon Him in truth.
      (PSALM 145:16-18)

ON FORGIVENESS

My desires chain me to evil
My decisions disappoint You daily
Release me from bitter bondage
Rescue me from the belly of Sheol
Forget my many sins
Raise me from death into life
Grant O Lord that I may be FORGIVENESS

✻   ✻   ✻   ✻   ✻

Ascend in your thoughts to Calvary and realize how much your sins cost... Is it possible that you will wound the head of the Lord again with the crown of thorns of your sins? Will you again nail Him to the Cross, pierce His side, and mock His longsuffering patience? Or did you not know that in sinning you participate in tormenting the Savior and will share the fate of His tormentors? But if you cease your sin and repent, then you will share in the power of His death. Choose one or the other: either crucify Christ and perish eternally, or be crucified together with Christ and share eternal life with Him.

THEOPHAN THE RECLUSE

TURNING THE HEART TO GOD

✳ ✳ ✳

✝ Your Father knows the things you have need of before you ask Him. In this manner, therefore, pray:
Our Father in heaven,
Hallowed be Your name.
Your kingdom come.
Your will be done
On earth as it is in heaven.
Give us this day our daily bread.
And forgive us our debts,
As we forgive our debtors.
And do not lead us into temptation,
But deliver us from the evil one.
For Yours is the kingdom and the power and the glory forever. Amen.
For if you forgive men their trespasses, your heavenly Father will also forgive you. But if you do not forgive men their trespasses, neither will your Father forgive your trespasses. (MATTHEW 6:8-15)

✝ To the Lord our God belong mercy and forgiveness, though we have rebelled against Him. (DANIEL 9:9)

✝ Therefore, as the elect of God, holy and beloved, put on tender mercies, kindness, humility, meekness, longsuffering; bearing with one another, and forgiving one another, if anyone has a complaint against another; even as Christ forgave you, so you also must do. (COLOSSIANS 3:13)

✝ You were bought at a price; therefore glorify God in your body and in your spirit, which are God's. (1 CORINTHIANS 6:20)

✝ Who is a God like You,
Pardoning iniquity
And passing over the transgression of the remnant of His heritage?

He does not retain His anger forever,
Because He delights in mercy.
He will again have compassion on us,
And will subdue our iniquities.
You will cast all our sins
Into the depths of the sea. (MICAH 7:18-19)

✝ I acknowledged my sin to You,
And my iniquity I have not hidden.
I said, "I will confess my transgressions
to the Lord,"
And You forgave the iniquity of my sin. (PSALM 32:5)

✝ If we confess our sins, He is faithful and just to forgive us our
sins and to cleanse us from all unrighteousness. (1 JOHN 1:9)

✝ And whenever you stand praying, if you have anything against
anyone, forgive him, that your Father in heaven may also forgive
you your trespasses. But if you do not forgive, neither will your
Father in heaven forgive your trespasses. (MARK 11:25)

✝ Take heed to yourselves. If your brother sins against you, rebuke
him; and if he repents, forgive him. And if he sins against you
seven times in a day, and seven times in a day returns to you,
saying, "I repent," you shall forgive him. (LUKE 17:3-4)

✝ Remember, O Lord, Your tender mercies and Your
lovingkindnesses,
For they are from of old.
Do not remember the sins of my youth, nor my transgressions;
According to Your mercy remember me,
For Your goodness' sake, O Lord.
(PSALM 25:6-7)

✝ Now having been set free from sin, and having become slaves
of God, you have your fruit to holiness, and the end, everlasting
life. (ROMANS 6:22)

ON SERVICE

My journey seeks the bruised and crushed
My fullness comes from lifting the needy
Help me understand that all are my neighbor
Adorn me with earnest love for all
Season my acts with mercy and grace
Sanctify my ministry of faith
Grant O Lord that I may be SERVICE

✸   ✸   ✸   ✸   ✸

What is the mark of a Christian? Faith working through love. What is the mark of love for God? Keeping His commandments in aim of His glory. What is the mark of love for one's neighbor? Not seeking one's own aims, but those of the beloved unto the benefit of both soul and body

BASIL THE GREAT

ON CHRISTIAN ETHICS

✳   ✳   ✳

✝   Then the King will say to those on His right hand, "Come, you blessed of My Father, inherit the kingdom prepared for you from the foundation of the world: for I was hungry and you gave Me food; I was thirsty and you gave Me drink; I was a stranger and you took Me in; I was naked and you clothed Me; I was sick and you visited Me; I was in prison and you came to Me." (MATTHEW 25:34-36)

✝   Above all things have fervent love for one another, for "love will cover a multitude of sins." *Be* hospitable to one another without grumbling. As each one has received a gift, minister it to one another, as good stewards of the manifold grace of God. (1 PETER 4:8-10)

✝   And He Himself gave some *to be* apostles, some prophets, some evangelists, and some pastors and teachers, for the equipping of the saints for the work of ministry, for the edifying of the body of Christ, till we all come to the unity of the faith and of the knowledge of the Son of God, to a perfect man, to the measure of the stature of the fullness of Christ. (EPHESIANS 4:11-13)

✝   Inasmuch as you did it to one of the least of these My brethren, you did it to Me. (MATTHEW 25:40)

✝   Pure and undefiled religion before God and the Father is this: to visit orphans and widows in their trouble, and to keep oneself unspotted from the world. (JAMES 1:27)

✝   Whoever desires to become great among you shall be your servant. And whoever of you desires to be first shall be slave of all. For even the Son of Man did not come to be served, but to serve, and to give His life a ransom for many. (MARK 10:43-45)

✝   By this we know love, because He laid down His life for us. And we also ought to lay down *our* lives for the brethren. But whoever has this world's goods, and sees his brother in need, and shuts up his heart from him, how does the love of God abide in him? My little children, let us not love in word or in tongue, but in deed and in truth. (1 JOHN 3:16-18)

✝ What *does it* profit, my brethren, if someone says he has faith but does not have works? Can faith save him? If a brother or sister is naked and destitute of daily food, and one of you says to them, "Depart in peace, be warmed and filled," but you do not give them the things which are needed for the body, what does it profit? Thus also faith by itself, if it does not have works, is dead. (JAMES 2:14-17)

✝ Give, and it will be given to you: good measure, pressed down, shaken together, and running over will be put into your bosom. For with the same measure that you use, it will be measured back to you. (LUKE 6:38)

✝ Whatever you do, do it heartily, as to the Lord and not to men, knowing that from the Lord you will receive the reward of the inheritance; for you serve the Lord Christ. (COLOSSIANS 3:23-24)

✝ *Let* each one *give* as he purposes in his heart, not grudgingly or of necessity; for God loves a cheerful giver. And God *is* able to make all grace abound toward you, that you, always having all sufficiency in all *things*, may have an abundance for every good work. (2 CORINTHIANS 9:7-8)

✝ *Let* nothing *be done* through selfish ambition or conceit, but in lowliness of mind let each esteem others better than himself. Let each of you look out not only for his own interests, but also for the interests of others. (PHILIPPIANS 2:3-4)

✝ If anyone serves Me, let him follow Me; and where I am, there My servant will be also. If anyone serves Me, him My Father will honor. (JOHN 12:26)

✝   So when He had washed their feet, taken His garments, and sat down again, He said to them, "Do you know what I have done to you? You call Me Teacher and Lord, and you say well, for so I am. If I then, your Lord and Teacher, have washed your feet, you also ought to wash one another's feet. For I have given you an example, that you should do as I have done to you. Most assuredly, I say to you, a servant is not greater than his master; nor is he who is sent greater than he who sent him. If you know these things, blessed are you if you do them." (JOHN 13:12-17)

✝   For though I am free from all *men*, I have made myself a servant to all, that I might win the more; to the weak I became as weak, that I might win the weak. I have become all things to all *men*, that I might by all means save some. Now this I do for the gospel's sake. (1 CORINTHIANS 9:19, 22-23)

ON MERCY

My life deserves eternal condemnation
My soul battles the shackles of iron
Receive me when I cry
Carry me out of my misery
Turn my punishment into salvation
Scent my garments with the fragrance of Lebanon
Grant O Lord that I may be MERCY

✳   ✳   ✳   ✳   ✳

Whoever has washed the feet of the saints will himself be cleansed in that dew; to the hand that has stretched out to give to the poor will the fruits of the trees themselves stretch out; the very footsteps of him who visited the sick in their affliction do the flowers make haste to crown with blooms, jostling to see which can be first to kiss his steps.

EPHREM THE SYRIAN

HYMNS ON PARADISE

✳ ✳ ✳

✝ When the kindness and the love of God our Savior toward man appeared, not by works of righteousness which we have done, but according to His mercy He saved us, through the washing of regeneration and renewing of the Holy Spirit. (TITUS 3:4-5)

✝ Be merciful, just as your Father also is merciful. (LUKE 6:36)

✝ The Lord your God is gracious and merciful, and will not turn His face from you if you return to Him. (2 CHRONICLES 30:9)

✝ To You, O Lord, I lift up my soul.
For You, Lord, are good, and ready to forgive,
And abundant in mercy to all those
who call upon You.
Give ear, O Lord, to my prayer;
And attend to the voice of my supplications.
In the day of my trouble I will call upon You,
For You will answer me. (PSALM 86:4-7)

✝ Hear me when I call, O God of my righteousness!
You have relieved me in my distress;
Have mercy on me, and hear my prayer. (PSALM 4:1)

✝ From the end of the earth I will cry to You,
When my heart is overwhelmed;
Lead me to the rock that is higher than I. (PSALM 61:2)

✝ I will lift up my eyes to the hills—
From whence comes my help?
My help comes from the Lord,
Who made heaven and earth. (PSALM 121:1-2)

✝ Through the Lord's mercies we are not consumed,
Because His compassions fail not.

They are new every morning;
Great is Your faithfulness. (LAMENTATIONS 3:22-23)

✝ He has shown you, O man, what is good;
And what does the Lord require of you
But to do justly,
To love mercy,
And to walk humbly with your God? (MICAH 6:8)

✝ The wicked borrows and does not repay,
But the righteous shows mercy and gives. (PSALM 37:21)

✝ In my distress I cried to the Lord,
And He heard me. (PSALM 120:1)

✝ O God, do not be far from me;
O my God, make haste to help me! (PSALM 71:12)

✝ Have mercy on me, O Lord, for I am weak;
O Lord, heal me, for my bones are troubled.
My soul also is greatly troubled;
But You, O Lord—how long?
Return, O Lord, deliver me!
Oh, save me for Your mercies' sake! (PSALM 6:2-4)

✝ So you, by the help of your God, return;
Observe mercy and justice,
And wait on your God continually. (HOSEA 12:6)

✝ I have trusted in Your mercy;
My heart shall rejoice in Your salvation.
I will sing to the Lord,
Because He has dealt bountifully with me.
(PSALM 13:5-6)

✝ To the Lord our God belong mercy and forgiveness, though we have rebelled against Him. (DANIEL 9:9)

✝ Blessed are the merciful,
For they shall obtain mercy. (MATTHEW 5:7)

ON LOVE

My person pursues praising You
My purpose payment of my debts
Inscribe me on the palms of Your hands
Kiss me with the kisses of Your mouth
Consecrate my heart, soul, and mind
Accept my sacrifice as a sweet aroma
Grant O Lord that I may be LOVE

✳ ✳ ✳ ✳ ✳

The life of the heart is love, while malice and enmity against our brother are the heart's death. The Lord keeps us on this earth in order for love for God and neighbor to completely penetrate our heart. This is what He expects from us all. This is, indeed, the purpose of the world's continued existence.

JOHN OF KRONSTADT

My Life in Christ

✺   ✺   ✺

✝ The first of all the commandments is: "Hear, O Israel, the Lord our God, the Lord is one. And you shall love the Lord your God with all your heart, with all your soul, with all your mind, and with all your strength." This is the first commandment. And the second, like it, is this: "You shall love your neighbor as yourself." There is no other commandment greater than these. (MARK 12:29-31)

✝ He who does not love does not know God, for God is love. (1 JOHN 4:8)

✝ Love suffers long and is kind; love does not envy; love does not parade itself, is not puffed up; does not behave rudely, does not seek its own, is not provoked, thinks no evil; does not rejoice in iniquity, but rejoices in the truth; bears all things, believes all things, hopes all things, endures all things. Love never fails. (1 CORINTHIANS 13:4-8)

✝ Walk worthy of the calling with which you were called, with all lowliness and gentleness, with longsuffering, bearing with one another in love. (EPHESIANS 4:1-2)

✝ For God so loved the world that He gave His only begotten Son, that whoever believes in Him should not perish but have everlasting life. (JOHN 3:16)

✝ And we know that all things work together for good to those who love God, to those who are the called according to His purpose. For whom He foreknew, He also predestined to be conformed to the image of His Son, that He might be the firstborn among many brethren. (ROMANS 8:28-29)

✝ And we have known and believed the love that God has for us. God is love, and he who abides in love abides in God, and God in him. (1 JOHN 4:16)

✝ A new commandment I give to you, that you love one another; as I have loved you, that you also love one another. By this all will know that you are My disciples, if you have love for one another. (JOHN 13:34-35)

✝ Therefore, as the elect of God, holy and beloved, put on tender mercies, kindness, humility, meekness, longsuffering; bearing with one another, and forgiving one another, if anyone has a complaint against another; even as Christ forgave you, so you also must do. But above all these things put on love, which is the bond of perfection. (COLOSSIANS 3:12-14)

✝ And now abide faith, hope, love, these three; but the greatest of these is love. (1 CORINTHIANS 13:13)

✝ Love your enemies, do good to those who hate you, bless those who curse you, and pray for those who spitefully use you. To him who strikes you on the one cheek, offer the other also. And from him who takes away your cloak, do not withhold your tunic either. Give to everyone who asks of you. And from him who takes away your goods do not ask them back. And just as you want men to do to you, you also do to them likewise. But if you love those who love you, what credit is that to you? For even sinners love those who love them. And if you do good to those who do good to you, what credit is that to you? For even sinners do the same. And if you lend to those from whom you hope to receive back, what credit is that to you? For even sinners lend to sinners to receive as much back. But love your enemies, do good, and lend, hoping for nothing in return; and your reward will be great, and you will be sons of the Most High. For He is kind to the unthankful and evil. Therefore be merciful, just as your Father also is merciful. (LUKE 6:27-36)

✝ Owe no one anything except to love one another, for he who loves another has fulfilled the law. (ROMANS 13:8)

✝ And above all things have fervent love for one another, for "love will cover a multitude of sins." (1 PETER 4:8)

✝ As the Father loved Me, I also have loved you; abide in My love. If you keep My commandments, you will abide in My love, just as I have kept My Father's commandments and abide in His love. These things I have spoken to you, that My joy may remain in you, and that your joy may be full. This is My commandment, that you love one another as I have loved you. Greater love has no one than this, than to lay down one's life for his friends. (JOHN 15:9-13)

✝ Beloved, since God loved us so much, we also ought to love one another. (1 JOHN 4:11)

✝ For I am persuaded that neither death nor life, nor angels nor principalities nor powers, nor things present nor things to come, nor height nor depth, nor any other created thing, shall be able to separate us from the love of God which is in Christ Jesus our Lord. (ROMANS 8:38-39)

✝ The Lord opens the eyes of the blind;
The Lord raises those who are bowed down;
The Lord loves the righteous. (PSALM 146:8)

✝ Let all that you do be done with love. (1 CORINTHIANS 16:14)

ON JOY

My heart discovers the paradise of bliss
My hunger satisfied by Your sweetness
Brighten me with the rays of dawn
Shelter me from the shadow of darkness
Extend my exaltation to everlasting
Permit my praise to climb the mountaintop
Grant O Lord that I may be JOY

✳ ✳ ✳ ✳ ✳

When the Spirit of God comes down to someone and overshadows him with the fullness of His presence, then that person's soul overflows with unspeakable joy, for the Holy Spirit fills with joy whatever He touches.

SERAPHIM OF SAROV

A Treasure of Russian Spirituality

✳   ✳   ✳

✝ And Mary said:
"My soul magnifies the Lord,
And my spirit has rejoiced in God my Savior.
For He has regarded the lowly
state of His maidservant;
For behold, henceforth all generations
will call me blessed.
For He who is mighty has done
great things for me,
And holy is His name.
And His mercy is on those who fear Him
From generation to generation.
He has shown strength with His arm;
He has scattered the proud in the
imagination of their hearts.
He has put down the mighty from their thrones,
And exalted the lowly.
He has filled the hungry with good things,
And the rich He has sent away empty.
He has helped His servant Israel,
In remembrance of His mercy,
As He spoke to our fathers,
To Abraham and to his seed forever."
(LUKE 1:46-55)

✝ You have put gladness in my heart. (PSALM 4:7)

✝ Rejoice in the Lord always. Again I will say, rejoice!
(PHILIPPIANS 4:4)

✝ But let all those rejoice who put their trust in You;
Let them ever shout for joy, because
You defend them;
Let those also who love Your name
Be joyful in You.
For You, O Lord, will bless the righteous;

With favor You will surround him as with a shield. (PSALM 5:11-12)

✝ You will show me the path of life;
In Your presence is fullness of joy;
At Your right hand are pleasures forevermore. (PSALM 16:11)

✝ Therefore my heart is glad, and my glory rejoices;
My flesh also will rest in hope. (PSALM 16:9)

✝ You have turned for me my mourning into dancing;
You have put off my sackcloth and clothed me with gladness.
(PSALM 30:11)

✝ His favor is for life;
Weeping may endure for a night,
But joy comes in the morning. (PSALM 30:5)

✝ The hope of the righteous will be gladness. (PROVERBS 10:28)

✝ My heart rejoices in the Lord;
My horn is exalted in the Lord.
I smile at my enemies,
Because I rejoice in Your salvation.
(1 SAMUEL 2:1)

✝ The Lord is my strength and song,
And He has become my salvation.
The voice of rejoicing and salvation
Is in the tents of the righteous;
The right hand of the Lord does valiantly.
The right hand of the Lord is exalted;
The right hand of the Lord does valiantly. (PSALM 118:14-16)

✝   This is the day the Lord has made;
We will rejoice and be glad in it. (PSALM 118:24)

✝   Until now you have asked nothing in My name. Ask, and you will receive, that your joy may be full. (JOHN 16:24)

✝   Glory in His holy name;
Let the hearts of those rejoice who seek the Lord! (1 CHRONICLES 16:10)

✝   The Lord is my strength and my shield;
My heart trusted in Him, and I am helped; Therefore my heart greatly rejoices,
And with my song I will praise Him.
(PSALM 28:7)

✝   And my soul shall be joyful in the Lord;
It shall rejoice in His salvation.
All my bones shall say,
"Lord, who is like You,
Delivering the poor from him who
is too strong for him,
Yes, the poor and the needy from him who plunders him?"
(PSALM 35:8-10)

✝   Our soul waits for the Lord;
He is our help and our shield.
For our heart shall rejoice in Him,
Because we have trusted in His holy name.
Let Your mercy, O Lord, be upon us,
Just as we hope in You. (PSALM 33:20-22)

✝   Therefore you now have sorrow; but I will see you again and
     your heart will rejoice, and your joy no one will take from you.
     (JOHN 16:22)

ON PEACE

My anguish drowns my gladness
My resting place forgotten
Receive me in Your midst
Hide me from my enemies
Eliminate my baseless fears
Parade my victorious salvation
Grant O Lord that I may be PEACE

✳ ✳ ✳ ✳ ✳

Be at peace with your own soul; then heaven and earth will be at peace with you. Enter eagerly into the treasure house that is within you, and so you will see the things that are in heaven; for there is but one single entry to them both. The ladder that leads to the kingdom is hidden within your soul. Flee from sin, dive into yourself, and in your soul you will discover the stairs by which to ascend.

ISAAC OF NINEVEH

ON ASCETICAL LIFE

✳   ✳   ✳

✝ Blessed are the peacemakers,
For they shall be called sons of God. (MATTHEW 5:9)

✝ The Lord will give strength to His people;
The Lord will bless His people with peace. (PSALM 29:11)

✝ The fruit of righteousness is sown in peace by those who make peace. (JAMES 3:18)

✝ Mercy and truth have met together;
Righteousness and peace have kissed. (PSALM 85:10)

✝ And let the peace of God rule in your hearts, to which also you were called in one body; and be thankful. (COLOSSIANS 3:15)

✝ Pursue peace with all people, and holiness, without which no one will see the Lord. (HEBREWS 12:14)

✝ Depart from evil and do good;
Seek peace and pursue it. (PSALM 34:14)

✝ Let him turn away from evil and do good; Let him seek peace and pursue it. (1 PETER 3:11)

✝ The Lord will fight for you, and you shall hold your peace. (EXODUS 14:14)

✝ Peace be with you; do not fear. (JUDGES 6:23)

✝ He has redeemed my soul in peace from the battle that was against me,

✝ For there were many against me. (PSALM 55:18)

✝ When a man's ways please the Lord,
He makes even his enemies to be at peace with him.
(PROVERBS 16:7)

✝ Go in peace. The presence of the Lord be with you on your way.
(JUDGES 18:6)

✝ In Me you may have peace. In the world you will have
tribulation; but be of good cheer, I have overcome the world.
(JOHN 16:33)

✝ He who is devoid of wisdom despises his neighbor,
But a man of understanding holds his peace. (PROVERBS
11:12)

✝ Lord, You will establish peace for us,
For You have also done all our works in us. (ISAIAH 26:12)

✝ Become complete. Be of good comfort, be of one mind, live
in peace; and the God of love and peace will be with you. (2
CORINTHIANS 13:11)

✝ Peace I leave with you, My peace I give to you; not as the world
gives do I give to you. Let not your heart be troubled, neither let
it be afraid. (JOHN 14:27)

ON LONGSUFFERING

My afflictions sink my head
My sorrow fills fountains with tears
Bring me to a place of rest
Quench me with water not gall
Lighten my heavy burden
Refresh my spirit unto eternity
Grant O Lord that I may be LONGSUFFERING

✳ ✳ ✳ ✳ ✳

Christ came as the radiance of God's glory to drive away the heavy fog that lay over the hearts of men. He came to grant comfort to the weary and distressed, and to those for whom, because of the abundance of their despair, life had come to seem like a night with no coming dawn. He came to bear the burden of all the hearts that were being crushed under the weight of worries and sufferings. The True Light came as the power of a new life in order to halt the stream of transgression spreading throughout humanity's being, and to lift up and deliver all those who were drowning in the oceans of darkness, and give new life to those who have been swept away in the current of death.

EPIPHANIUS OF WADI EL NATRUN

SO GREAT A SALVATION

✳ ✳ ✳

✝   My soul melts from heaviness;
Strengthen me according to Your word. (PSALM 119:28)
Have you not known?
Have you not heard?
The everlasting God, the Lord,
The Creator of the ends of the earth,
Neither faints nor is weary.
His understanding is unsearchable.
He gives power to the weak,
And to those who have no might
He increases strength.
Even the youths shall faint and be weary,
And the young men shall utterly fall,
But those who wait on the Lord
Shall renew their strength;
They shall mount up with wings like eagles,
They shall run and not be weary,
They shall walk and not faint.
(ISAIAH 40:28-31)

✝   And let us not grow weary while doing good, for in due season we shall reap if we do not lose heart. (GALATIANS 6:9)

✝   Therefore we do not lose heart. Even though our outward man is perishing, yet the inward man is being renewed day by day. (2 CORINTHIANS 4:16)

✝   Therefore, my beloved brethren, be steadfast, immovable, always abounding in the work of the Lord, knowing that your labor is not in vain in the Lord. (1 CORINTHIANS 15:58)

✝   When you pass through the waters,
I will be with you;
And through the rivers, they shall not overflow you.
When you walk through the fire, you shall not be burned,
Nor shall the flame scorch you. (ISAIAH 43:2)

✝   In the world you will have tribulation; but be of good cheer, I have overcome the world. (JOHN 16:33)

✝   My brethren, count it all joy when you fall into various trials, knowing that the testing of your faith produces patience. But let patience have its perfect work, that you may be perfect and complete, lacking nothing. (JAMES 1:2-4)

✝   We also glory in tribulations, knowing that tribulation produces perseverance; and perseverance, character; and character, hope. (ROMANS 5:3-4)

✝   Many will be offended, will betray one another, and will hate one another. Then many false prophets will rise up and deceive many. And because lawlessness will abound, the love of many will grow cold. But he who endures to the end shall be saved. (MATTHEW 24:10-13)

✝   Let us lay aside every weight, and the sin which so easily ensnares us, and let us run with endurance the race that is set before us, looking unto Jesus, the author and finisher of our faith, who for the joy that was set before Him endured the cross, despising the shame, and has sat down at the right hand of the throne of God. For consider Him who endured such hostility from sinners against Himself, lest you become weary and discouraged in your souls. (HEBREWS 12:1-3)

✝   To everything there is a season,
A time for every purpose under heaven:
A time to plant,
And a time to pluck what is planted;
A time to weep,
And a time to laugh;
A time to mourn,
And a time to dance.
(ECCLESIASTES 3:1-2,4)

ON KINDNESS

My arms embrace my sister and brother
My heart knows all deserve affection
Instruct me in the way I should walk
Inspire me with the memory of Your crucifixion
Anchor my thoughts in compassion
Enrobe my actions with hospitality
Grant O Lord that I may be KINDNESS

✳ ✳ ✳ ✳ ✳

Blessed is he who purchases Christ with all his belongings and has, as his only possession, the cross, which he raises on high. Blessed is he who, administering his cleanly-gained possessions, extends God's hand to those who are in need.

GREGORY THE THEOLOGIAN

On God and Man: Blessings of Various Lives

✴   ✴   ✴

✝ Be kind to one another, tenderhearted, forgiving one another, even as God in Christ forgave you. (EPHESIANS 4:32)

✝ Comfort each other and edify one another. (1 THESSALONIANS 5:11)

✝ Do not forget to entertain strangers, for by so doing some have unwittingly entertained angels. (HEBREWS 13:2)

✝ You must support the weak. And remember the words of the Lord Jesus, that He said, "It is more blessed to give than to receive." (ACTS 20:35)

✝ Remember the prisoners as if chained with them – those who are mistreated – since you yourselves are in the body also. (HEBREWS 13:3)

✝ Assuredly, I say to you, inasmuch as you did it to one of the least of these My brethren, you did it to Me. (MATTHEW 25:40)

✝ For God is not unjust to forget your work and labor of love which you have shown toward His name, in that you have ministered to the saints, and do minister. (HEBREWS 6:10)

✝ Let love be without hypocrisy. Abhor what is evil. Cling to what is good. Be kindly affectionate to one another with brotherly love, in honor giving preference to one another; not lagging in diligence, fervent in spirit, serving the Lord; rejoicing in hope, patient in tribulation, continuing steadfastly in prayer; distributing to the needs of the saints, given to hospitality. (ROMANS 12:9-12)

✝ I have gone astray like a lost sheep;
Seek Your servant,
For I do not forget Your commandments. (PSALM 119:176)

✝   "Now, therefore," says the Lord,
     "Turn to Me with all your heart,
     With fasting, with weeping, and with mourning."
     So rend your heart, and not your garments;
     Return to the Lord your God,
     For He is gracious and merciful,
     Slow to anger, and of great kindness;
     And He relents from doing harm. (JOEL 2:12-13)

ON GOODNESS

My tears wash Your feet
My fragrant oil anoints Your head
Regard me in my lowly state
Introduce me to the strength of Your arm
Transform my barrenness to rejoicing
Hearten my labor
Grant O Lord that I may be GOODNESS

✳   ✳   ✳   ✳   ✳

Inner work with labor of heart brings purity, and purity brings true quiet of heart, and such quiet brings humility, and humility renders a person the dwelling-place of God, and from this dwelling-place the evil demons are banished, together with the devil who is their captain, as well as their unworthy passions. Then, that person is found to be a temple of God, sanctified, illumined, purified, graceful, filled with every fragrance and goodness and gladness; and that person is found to be a God-bearer.

BARSANUPHIUS OF GAZA

LETTERS FROM THE DESERT

❋   ❋   ❋

✝ Oh, taste and see that the Lord is good;
Blessed is the man who trusts in Him! (PSALM 34:8)

✝ He satisfies the longing soul,
And fills the hungry soul with goodness. (PSALM 107:9)

✝ The Lord is good,
A stronghold in the day of trouble;
And He knows those who trust in Him. (NAHUM 1:7)

✝ And we know that all things work together for good to those
who love God, to those who are the called according to His
purpose. (ROMANS 8:28)

✝ Blessed be the God and Father of our Lord Jesus Christ, the
Father of mercies and God of all comfort, who comforts us in
all our tribulation, that we may be able to comfort those who
are in any trouble, with the comfort with which we ourselves are
comforted by God. (2 CORINTHIANS 1:3-4)

✝ But do not forget to do good and to share, for with such
sacrifices God is well pleased. (HEBREWS 13:16)

✝ Bear one another's burdens, and thereby fulfill the law of Christ.
(GALATIANS 6:2)

✝ The generous soul will be made rich,
And he who waters will also be watered himself.
The people will curse him who withholds grain,
But blessing will be on the head of him who sells it.
He who earnestly seeks good finds favor,
But trouble will come to him who seeks evil.
(PROVERBS 11:25-27)

✝ You are the light of the world. A city that is set on a hill cannot
be hidden. Nor do they light a lamp and put it under a basket,

but on a lampstand, and it gives light to all who are in the house. Let your light so shine before men, that they may see your good works and glorify your Father in heaven. (MATTHEW 5:14-16)

✝   Blessed be the Lord my Rock,
My lovingkindness and my fortress,
My high tower and my deliverer,
My shield and the One in whom I take refuge.
(PSALM 144:1-2)

ON FAITHFULNESS

My branch has broken from the olive tree
My day of desiccation nears
Graft me in that I might live
Enliven me by the still waters
Remember my place among the green pastures
Ripen my fruits for the harvest
Grant O Lord that I may be FAITHFULNESS

* * * * *

We were overwhelmed by our sins; we had fallen away from You into the depths of darkness, and Your good Spirit was moving over us, ready to bring help when the time was due. You made just men of sinners and set them apart from the wicked; You established the authority of Your Book between those above, who would be obedient to You, and those beneath, who would be made subject to them; and You gathered all the faithless together into one body, so that the earnest devotion of the faithful might be clearly seen and they might bear You fruit in works of mercy, by distributing their worldly wealth to the poor in order to acquire heavenly riches for themselves. You willed that the faithful, by providing them with what they need for temporal use, should do good works that would bear fruit in the future life.

AUGUSTINE OF HIPPO

On Grace and Free Will

* * *

✝ Trust in the Lord, and do good;
Dwell in the land, and feed on His faithfulness. (PSALM 37:3)

✝ Through the Lord's mercies we are not consumed,
Because His compassions fail not.
They are new every morning;
Great is Your faithfulness.
(LAMENTATIONS 3:22-23)

✝ Your mercy, O Lord, is in the heavens;
Your faithfulness reaches to the clouds.
(PSALM 36:5)

✝ Lord, lift up the light of Your countenance upon us.
You have put gladness in my heart.
I will both lie down in peace, and sleep;
For You alone, O Lord, make me dwell in safety.
(PSALM 4:6-8)

✝ Know the God of your father, and serve Him with a loyal heart
and with a willing mind; for the Lord searches all hearts and
understands all the intent of the thoughts. If you seek Him, He
will be found by you; but if you forsake Him, He will cast you
off forever. (1 CHRONICLES 28:9)

✝ No one can serve two masters; for either he will hate the one
and love the other, or else he will be loyal to the one and despise
the other. You cannot serve God and mammon. (MATTHEW
6:24)

✝ Therefore know that the Lord your God, He is God, the faithful
God who keeps covenant and mercy for a thousand generations
with those who love Him and keep His commandments
(DEUTERONOMY 7:9)

✝ Remember now, O Lord, I pray, how I have walked before You in truth and with a loyal heart, and have done what was good in Your sight. (2 KINGS 20:3)

✝   Oh, love the Lord, all you His saints!
For the Lord preserves the faithful,
And fully repays the proud person.
(PSALM 31:23)

✝   Preserve me, O God, for in You I put my trust.
O my soul, you have said to the Lord,
"You are my Lord,
My goodness is nothing apart from You."
(PSALM 16:1-2)

✝   How precious is Your lovingkindness, O God!
Therefore the children of men put their trust under the shadow
of Your wings.
They are abundantly satisfied with the
fullness of Your house,
And You give them drink from
the river of Your pleasures.
For with You is the fountain of life;
In Your light we see light. (PSALM 36:7-9)

ON GENTLENESS

My feet stamp the sand
My hair bounces with the breeze
Shield me from the coming waves
Secure me upon the cliffs
Grasp my hand
Calm my senses
Grant O Lord that I may be GENTLENESS

✳ ✳ ✳ ✳ ✳

Let your baptism remain as weaponry, faith as a helmet, love as a spear, endurance as armor, your works as a down-payment on your wages, so that you may receive the just back-pay. Therefore be patient with one another in gentleness, so that God may be with you.

IGNATIUS OF ANTIOCH

LETTER TO POLYCARP

✳   ✳   ✳

✝ The Lord is my shepherd;
I shall not want.
He makes me to lie down in green pastures;
He leads me beside the still waters.
He restores my soul;
He leads me in the paths of righteousness
For His name's sake.
Yea, though I walk through the valley of the shadow of death,
I will fear no evil;
For You are with me;
Your rod and Your staff, they comfort me. (PSALM 23:1-4)

✝ Come to Me, all you who labor and are heavy laden, and I
will give you rest. Take My yoke upon you and learn from
Me, for I am gentle and lowly in heart, and you will find rest
for your souls. For My yoke is easy and My burden is light.
(MATTHEW 11:28-30)

✝ You have also given me the shield of Your salvation;
Your gentleness has made me great.
(2 SAMUEL 22:36)

✝ A soft answer turns away wrath,
But a harsh word stirs up anger.
A wholesome tongue is a tree of life,
But perverseness in it breaks the spirit. (PROVERBS 15:1,4)

✝ A servant of the Lord must not quarrel but be gentle to all. (2
TIMOTHY 2:24)
You have also given me the shield of Your salvation;
Your right hand has held me up, Your gentleness has made me
great. (PSALM 18:35)

✝ Because your heart was tender, and you humbled yourself before
the Lord when you heard what I spoke against this place and
against its inhabitants, that they would become a desolation and

a curse, and you tore your clothes and wept before Me, I also have heard you. (2 CHRONICLES 34:27)

✝ Let your gentleness be known to all men. The Lord is at hand. (PHILIPPIANS 4:5)

✝ But the wisdom that is from above is first pure, then peaceable, gentle, willing to yield, full of mercy and good fruits, without partiality and without hypocrisy. (JAMES 3:17)

✝ He will feed His flock like a shepherd;
He will gather the lambs with His arm,
And carry them in His bosom,
And gently lead those who are with young. (ISAIAH 40:11)

✝ Lord, my heart is not haughty,
Nor my eyes lofty.
Neither do I concern myself with great matters,
Nor with things too profound for me.
Surely I have calmed and quieted my soul,
Like a weaned child with his mother;
Like a weaned child is my soul within me. (PSALM 131:1-2)

ON SELF-CONTROL

My passions burn as a forest fire
My lusts endless as the crashing waves
Force me to hate the devil's delicacies
Satisfy me with bitter herbs
Purify my lips
Curb my desires
Grant O Lord that I may be SELF-CONTROL

* * * * *

It is absolutely necessary for one who hopes to please God and to be acceptable and pure, not to pursue a relaxed and slippery and dissolute life, but a laborious life, groaning with much toil and sweat; for no one is crowned, Paul says, "unless he competes according to the rules." And elsewhere he says, "every athlete exercises self-control in all things," in speech and in sight, avoiding shameful words, abuse, blasphemy, and obscenity. From Paul's words we learn that even if trials are not brought to us from somewhere outside, we must exercise ourselves every day with fasting, austerity, cheap nourishment, and frugal table, always avoiding sumptuousness; otherwise we cannot please God.

JOHN CHRYSOSTOM

On Wealth and Poverty

✳   ✳   ✳

✝ Do you not know that those who run in a race all run, but one receives the prize? Run in such a way that you may obtain it. And everyone who competes for the prize is temperate in all things. Now they do it to obtain a perishable crown, but we for an imperishable crown. Therefore I run thus: not with uncertainty. Thus I fight: not as one who beats the air. But I discipline my body and bring it into subjection. (1 CORINTHIANS 9:24-27)

✝ Those who are Christ's have crucified the flesh with its passions and desires. If we live in the Spirit, let us also walk in the Spirit. (GALATIANS 5:24-25)

✝ Humble yourselves under the mighty hand of God, that He may exalt you in due time, casting all your care upon Him, for He cares for you. Be sober, be vigilant; because your adversary the devil walks about like a roaring lion, seeking whom he may devour. Resist him, steadfast in the faith. (1 PETER 5:6-9)

✝ Better is a little with the fear of the Lord,
Than great treasure with trouble.
Better is a dinner of herbs where love is,
Than a fatted calf with hatred.
(PROVERBS 15:16-17)

✝ Take heed and beware of covetousness, for one's life does not consist in the abundance of the things he possesses. (LUKE 12:15)

✝ Giving all diligence, add to your faith virtue, to virtue knowledge, to knowledge self-control, to self-control perseverance, to perseverance godliness, to godliness brotherly kindness, and to brotherly kindness love. For if these things are yours and abound, you will be neither barren nor unfruitful in the knowledge of our Lord Jesus Christ. For he who lacks these things is shortsighted, even to blindness, and has forgotten that he was cleansed from his old sins. (2 PETER 1:5-9)

✝   He who is slow to anger is better than the mighty,
And he who rules his spirit than he who takes a city.
(PROVERBS 16:32)

✝   Set a guard, O Lord, over my mouth;
Keep watch over the door of my lips.
Do not incline my heart to any evil thing,
To practice wicked works
With men who work iniquity;
And do not let me eat of their delicacies.
(PSALM 141:3-4)

✝   For the grace of God that brings salvation has appeared to all men, teaching us that, denying ungodliness and worldly lusts, we should live soberly, righteously, and godly in the present age, looking for the blessed hope and glorious appearing of our great God and Savior Jesus Christ, who gave Himself for us, that He might redeem us from every lawless deed and purify for Himself His own special people, zealous for good works. (TITUS 2:11-14)

✝   He who guards his mouth preserves his life,
But he who opens wide his lips shall have destruction.
(PROVERBS 13:3)

✝   And we labor, working with our own hands. Being reviled, we bless; being persecuted, we endure; being defamed, we entreat. We have been made as the filth of the world, the offscouring of all things until now. (1 CORINTHIANS 4:12-13)

ON POVERTY

My sumptuous feast spoils before my eyes
My treasures now the abode of myriad moths
Liberate me of this world's worthlessness
Endow me with keys to Your kingdom
Set my eyes on that which does not fail
Retain my wealth in paradise
Grant O Lord that I may be POVERTY

❋   ❋   ❋   ❋   ❋

Unless each one of you shall hate all nature of earthly possessions, and renounces them and all their works with all his heart, and stretches out the hands of his heart to heaven, to the Father of all, he cannot be saved. But if he does what I have said, God will have mercy upon him for his labor, and will grant him that invisible fire which will burn up all impurity from him, and purifies his mind. Then, the Holy Spirit will dwell in us, and Jesus will abide with us, and so we shall be able to worship God as is proper. But as long as we have peace with the natures of the world, we are enemies of God and of His angels and of all His saints.

ANTONY THE GREAT

THE LETTERS OF ST. ANTONY THE GREAT

✳ ✳ ✳

✝ Blessed are you poor,
For yours is the kingdom of God. (LUKE 6:21)

✝ You know the grace of our Lord Jesus Christ, that though He was rich, yet for your sakes He became poor, that you through His poverty might become rich. (2 CORINTHIANS 8:9)

✝ If you want to be perfect, go, sell what you have and give to the poor, and you will have treasure in heaven; and come, follow Me. (MATTHEW 19:21)

✝ He saves the needy from the sword,
From the mouth of the mighty,
And from their hand.
So the poor have hope,
And injustice shuts her mouth. (JOB 5:15-16)

✝ Do not fear, little flock, for it is your Father's good pleasure to give you the kingdom. Sell what you have and give alms; provide yourselves money bags which do not grow old, a treasure in the heavens that does not fail, where no thief approaches nor moth destroys. For where your treasure is, there your heart will be also. (LUKE 12:32-34)

✝ Lay aside all filthiness and overflow of wickedness, and receive with meekness the implanted word, which is able to save your souls. (JAMES 1:21)

✝ Blessed are the poor in spirit,
For theirs is the kingdom of heaven. (MATTHEW 5:3)

✝ Listen, my beloved brethren: Has God not chosen the poor of this world to be rich in faith and heirs of the kingdom which He promised to those who love Him? (JAMES 2:5)

✝ Go your way, sell whatever you have and give to the poor, and you will have treasure in heaven; and come, take up the cross, and follow Me. (MARK 10:21)

✝   By this we know love, because He laid down His life for us. And we also ought to lay down our lives for the brethren. But whoever has this world's goods, and sees his brother in need, and shuts up his heart from him, how does the love of God abide in him? (1 JOHN 3:16-17)

ON OBEDIENCE

My delight rests in Your commandments
My ears hearken to Your will
Point me toward the narrow gate
Accompany me in bearing my cross
Sprinkle my journey with suffering
Straighten my path that I may find the kingdom
Grant O Lord that I may be OBEDIENCE

✳ ✳ ✳ ✳ ✳

He gave us His holy commandments as if, we might say, He had given us tools, with faith in Him being as it were a kind of craftsman. So we are the vessels, faith is the worker, the commandments the tools through which the Word as Carpenter reforms and remakes the workers of His commandments, such that through their operation we may be purified and illumined, progressing by grace of the Spirit in the knowledge of the mysteries of the Kingdom of Heaven.

SYMEON THE NEW THEOLOGIAN

ON THE MYSTICAL LIFE

✳   ✳   ✳

✝ Then one of them, a lawyer, asked Him a question, testing Him, and saying, "Teacher, which is the great commandment in the law?" Jesus said to him, "'You shall love the Lord your God with all your heart, with all your soul, and with all your mind.' This is the first and great commandment. And the second is like it: 'You shall love your neighbor as yourself.' On these two commandments hang all the Law and the Prophets." (MATTHEW 22:35-40)

✝ I will never forget Your precepts,
For by them You have given me life.
(PSALM 119:93)

✝ Therefore God also has highly exalted Him and given Him the name which is above every name, that at the name of Jesus every knee should bow, of those in heaven, and of those on earth, and of those under the earth, and that every tongue should confess that Jesus Christ is Lord, to the glory of God the Father. (PHILIPPIANS 2:9-11)

✝ Do not labor for the food which perishes, but for the food which endures to everlasting life, which the Son of Man will give you, because God the Father has set His seal on Him. (JOHN 6:27)

✝ Therefore you shall love the Lord your God, and keep His charge, His statutes, His judgments, and His commandments always. (DEUTERONOMY 11:1)

✝ Imitate those who through faith and patience inherit the promises. (HEBREWS 6:12)

✝ As the Father loved Me, I also have loved you; abide in My love. (JOHN 15:9)

✝ Children, obey your parents in the Lord, for this is

right. "Honor your father and mother," which is the first commandment with promise: "that it may be well with you and you may live long on the earth." (EPHESIANS 6:1-3)

✝ Therefore lay aside all filthiness and overflow of wickedness, and receive with meekness the implanted word, which is able to save your souls. But be doers of the word, and not hearers only, deceiving yourselves. For if anyone is a hearer of the word and not a doer, he is like a man observing his natural face in a mirror; for he observes himself, goes away, and immediately forgets what kind of man he was. But he who looks into the perfect law of liberty and continues in it, and is not a forgetful hearer but a doer of the work, this one will be blessed in what he does. (JAMES 1:21-25)

✝ A man's heart plans his way,
But the Lord directs his steps. (PROVERBS 16:9)

✝ This is love, that we walk according to His commandments. This is the commandment, that as you have heard from the beginning, you should walk in it. (2 JOHN 1:6)

✝ Show me Your ways, O Lord;
Teach me Your paths.
Lead me in Your truth and teach me,
For You are the God of my salvation;
On You I wait all the day. (PSALM 25:4-5)

✝ Teach me to do Your will,
For You are my God;
Your Spirit is good.
Lead me in the land of uprightness.
(PSALM 143:10)

ON PURITY

My hands linger in filth
My bed amidst swine
Make me like one of Your hired servants
Give me a ring for my hand and sandals for my feet
Cover my nakedness with a white robe
Crowd my house with music and dancing
Grant O Lord that I may be PURITY

Holiness of body is the abstention from all shameful things and from all lawless deeds, while holiness of soul is to keep the faith in God whole, neither adding nor subtracting from it: for godliness becomes darkened and obscured by bodily impurity, and becomes broken and spoilt, not being whole, when falseness enters the soul; but it will be preserved in beauty and due measure, when truth is continually in the soul and holiness in the body.

IRENAEUS OF LYONS

ON THE APOSTOLIC PREACHING

✳   ✳   ✳

✝ Let us walk properly, as in the day, not in revelry and drunkenness, not in lewdness and lust, not in strife and envy. But put on the Lord Jesus Christ, and make no provision for the flesh, to fulfill its lusts. (ROMANS 13:13-14)

✝ Therefore put to death your members which are on the earth: fornication, uncleanness, passion, evil desire, and covetousness, which is idolatry. (COLOSSIANS 3:5)

✝ For this is the will of God, your sanctification: that you should abstain from sexual immorality; that each of you should know how to possess his own vessel in sanctification and honor, not in passion of lust, like the Gentiles who do not know God; that no one should take advantage of and defraud his brother in this matter, because the Lord is the avenger of all such, as we also forewarned you and testified. For God did not call us to uncleanness, but in holiness. Therefore he who rejects this does not reject man, but God, who has also given us His Holy Spirit. (1 THESSALONIANS 4:3-8)

✝ Beloved, I beg you as sojourners and pilgrims, abstain from fleshly lusts which war against the soul, having your conduct honorable. (1 PETER 2:11-12)

✝ All things are lawful for me, but all things are not helpful. All things are lawful for me, but I will not be brought under the power of any. Foods for the stomach and the stomach for foods, but God will destroy both it and them. Now the body is not for sexual immorality but for the Lord, and the Lord for the body. (1 CORINTHIANS 6:12-13)

✝ Behold what manner of love the Father has bestowed on us, that we should be called children of God! Therefore the world does not know us, because it did not know Him. Beloved, now we are children of God; and it has not yet been revealed what we shall be, but we know that when He is revealed, we shall be like Him, for we shall see Him as He is. And everyone who has

this hope in Him purifies himself, just as He is pure.
(1 JOHN 3:1-3)

✝   Lord, who may abide in Your tabernacle?
Who may dwell in Your holy hill?
He who walks uprightly,
And works righteousness,
And speaks the truth in his heart;
He who does not backbite with his tongue,
Nor does evil to his neighbor,
Nor does he take up a reproach against his friend.
(PSALM 15:1-3)

✝   Flee also youthful lusts; but pursue righteousness, faith, love,
peace with those who call on the Lord out of a pure heart. (2
TIMOTHY 2:22)

✝   Woe to you, scribes and Pharisees, hypocrites! For you cleanse
the outside of the cup and dish, but inside they are full of
extortion and self-indulgence. Blind Pharisee, first cleanse the
inside of the cup and dish, that the outside of them may be
clean also. (MATTHEW 23:27-28)

✝   Do you not know that your body is the temple of the Holy
Spirit who is in you, whom you have from God, and you are not
your own? For you were bought at a price; therefore glorify God
in your body and in your spirit, which are God's.
(1 CORINTHIANS 6:19-20)

✝   Do not love the world or the things in the world. If anyone
loves the world, the love of the Father is not in him. For all that
is in the world—the lust of the flesh, the lust of the eyes, and
the pride of life—is not of the Father but is of the world. And
the world is passing away, and the lust of it; but he who does the
will of God abides forever. (1 JOHN 2:15-17)

✝ Who may ascend into the hill of the Lord?
Or who may stand in His holy place?
He who has clean hands and a pure heart,
Who has not lifted up his soul to an idol,
Nor sworn deceitfully.
He shall receive blessing from the Lord,
And righteousness from the God of his salvation.
(PSALM 24:3-5)

ON WISDOM

My lamp burns as I contemplate Your love
My hope to understand its height and depth
Tell me why I mean so much to You
Send me Your Spirit as my teacher
Remove my thorns of pride and arrogance
Crown my head with the oil of Your grace
Grant O Lord that I may be WISDOM

* * * * *

A Christian receives divine wisdom in three ways: by the commandments, teachings, and faith. The commandments free the mind from passions. Teachings lead it to true knowledge of nature. Faith leads to the contemplation of the Holy Trinity.

MAXIMUS THE CONFESSOR

CHAPTERS ON LOVE

✷   ✷   ✷

✝ The fear of the Lord is the beginning of wisdom,
And the knowledge of the Holy One is understanding.
(PROVERBS 9:10)

✝ Oh, the depth of the riches both of the wisdom and knowledge
of God! How unsearchable are His judgments and His ways
past finding out! (ROMANS 11:33)

✝ One thing I have desired of the Lord,
That will I seek:
That I may dwell in the house of the Lord
All the days of my life,
To behold the beauty of the Lord,
And to inquire in His temple. (PSALM 27:4)

✝ But the wisdom that is from above is first pure, then peaceable,
gentle, willing to yield, full of mercy and good fruits, without
partiality and without hypocrisy. (JAMES 3:17)

✝ See then that you walk circumspectly, not as fools but as wise,
redeeming the time, because the days are evil. Therefore do
not be unwise, but understand what the will of the Lord is.
(EPHESIANS 5:15-17)

✝ How much better to get wisdom than gold!
And to get understanding is to be chosen rather than silver.
(PROVERBS 16:16)

✝ For God gives wisdom and knowledge and joy to a man who
is good in His sight; but to the sinner He gives the work of
gathering and collecting, that he may give to him who is good

before God. This also is vanity and grasping for the wind. (ECCLESIASTES 2:26)

✝ Therefore whoever hears these sayings of Mine, and does them, I will liken him to a wise man who built his house on the rock: and the rain descended, the floods came, and the winds blew and beat on that house; and it did not fall, for it was founded on the rock. (MATTHEW 7:24-25)

✝ If any of you lacks wisdom, let him ask of God, who gives to all liberally and without reproach, and it will be given to him. (JAMES 1:5)

✝ The fear of the Lord is the beginning of wisdom;
A good understanding have all those
who do His commandments.
His praise endures forever.
(PSALM 111:10)

ON COURAGE

My trembling fills the blackness
My foe listens for my breath
Array me with Your armor
Gird me with Your sword
Magnify my battle cry
Guide my hands to pierce his neck
Grant O Lord that I may be COURAGE

✻   ✻   ✻   ✻   ✻

A lack of courage is an immature disposition in an aged, prideful soul. Faint-heartedness is a lack of faith that is a result of expecting the unexpected. Being afraid is the practice of danger before it happens. Or another way, fear is a quivering feeling of the heart, anxious and worried by unknown dangers. Fear is the loss of resolve. The one who has overcome fear has certainly devoted his body and soul to God.

JOHN CLIMACUS

LADDER OF DIVINE ASCENT

* * *

✝ Whenever I am afraid,
I will trust in You.
In God (I will praise His word),
In God I have put my trust;
I will not fear. (PSALM 56:3-4)

✝ But the Lord is with me as a mighty, awesome One. Therefore my persecutors will stumble, and will not prevail. (JEREMIAH 20:11)

✝ Be strong and of good courage, do not fear nor be afraid of them; for the Lord your God, He is the One who goes with you. He will not leave you nor forsake you. (DEUTERONOMY 31:6)

✝ For God has not given us a spirit of fear, but of power and of love and of a sound mind. (2 TIMOTHY 1:7)

✝ Only be strong and very courageous, that you may observe to do according to all the law which Moses My servant commanded you; do not turn from it to the right hand or to the left, that you may prosper wherever you go. (JOSHUA 1:7)

✝ Be of good courage,
And He shall strengthen your heart,
All you who hope in the Lord. (PSALM 31:24)

✝ Have I not commanded you? Be strong and of good courage; do not be afraid, nor be dismayed, for the Lord your God is with you wherever you go. (JOSHUA 1:9)

✝ If God is for us, who can be against us? (ROMANS 8:31)

✝ No temptation has overtaken you except such as is common to man; but God is faithful, who will not allow you to be tempted beyond what you are able, but with the temptation will also make the way of escape, that you may be able to bear it. (1 CORINTHIANS 10:13)

✝ Peace I leave with you, My peace I give to you; not as the world gives do I give to you. Let not your heart be troubled, neither let it be afraid. (JOHN 14:27)

✝ For the Lord your God is He who goes with you, to fight for you against your enemies, to save you. (DEUTERONOMY 20:4)

✝ The name of the Lord is a strong tower;
The righteous run to it and are safe.
(PROVERBS 18:10)

✝ I would have lost heart, unless I had believed
That I would see the goodness of the Lord
In the land of the living.
Wait on the Lord;
Be of good courage,
And He shall strengthen your heart;
Wait, I say, on the Lord!
(PSALM 27:13-14)

ON STRENGTH

My feet stumble on rocks
My heart fails amidst tribulation
Recover me when I fall
Establish me on Your holy mountain
Elevate my head above my enemies
Fortify my members so I will not be shaken
Grant O Lord that I may be STRENGTH

✳ ✳ ✳ ✳ ✳

We have within us deeply rooted weaknesses, passions, and defects. This cannot all be cut out with one sharp motion, but patience, persistence, care, and attention. The path leading to perfection is long. Pray to God so that He will strengthen you. Patiently accept your falls and, having stood up, immediately run to God, not remaining in that place where you have fallen. Do not despair if you keep falling into your old sins. Many of them are strong because they have received the force of habit. Only with the passage of time and with fervor will they be conquered. Do not let anything deprive you of hope.

NECTARIOS OF AEGINA

PATH TO HAPPINESS

✳   ✳   ✳

✝ My flesh and my heart fail;
But God is the strength of my heart and my portion forever.
(PSALM 73:26)

✝ The Lord will give strength to His people;
The Lord will bless His people with peace. (PSALM 29:11)

✝ Fear not, for I am with you;
Be not dismayed, for I am your God.
I will strengthen you,
Yes, I will help you,
I will uphold you with My righteous right hand.
(ISAIAH 41:10)

✝ The Lord is my strength and song,
And He has become my salvation;
He is my God, and I will praise Him;
My father's God, and I will exalt Him.
(EXODUS 15:2)

✝ Both riches and honor come from You,
And You reign over all.
In Your hand is power and might;
In Your hand it is to make great
And to give strength to all.
(1 CHRONICLES 29:12)

✝ But the salvation of the righteous is from the Lord;
He is their strength in the time of trouble. (PSALM 37:39)

✝ The Lord your God in your midst,
The Mighty One, will save;
He will rejoice over you with gladness,
He will quiet you with His love,
He will rejoice over you with singing. (ZEPHANIAH 3:17)

✝ Do not sorrow, for the joy of the Lord is your strength.
(NEHEMIAH 8:10)

✝ I will love You, O Lord, my strength.
The Lord is my rock and my fortress
and my deliverer;
My God, my strength, in whom I will trust;
My shield and the horn of my salvation, my stronghold.
(PSALM 18:1-2)

✝ If anyone speaks, let him speak as the oracles of God. If anyone
ministers, let him do it as with the ability which God supplies,
that in all things God may be glorified through Jesus Christ,
to whom belong the glory and the dominion forever and ever.
Amen. (1 PETER 4:11)

✝ The Lord is my light and my salvation;
Whom shall I fear?
The Lord is the strength of my life;
Of whom shall I be afraid? (PSALM 27:1)

✝ Be strong in the Lord and in the power of His might.
(EPHESIANS 6:10)

✝ In the day when I cried out, You answered me,
And made me bold with strength in my soul. (PSALM 138:3)

✝ The Lord God is my strength;
He will make my feet like deer's feet,
And He will make me walk on my high hills.
(HABAKKUK 3:19)

✝ God is our refuge and strength,
A very present help in trouble.
Therefore we will not fear,
Even though the earth be removed,

✝ And though the mountains be carried into the midst of the sea;
Though its waters roar and be troubled,
Though the mountains shake with its swelling.
(PSALM 46:1-3)

✝ Behold, God is my salvation,
I will trust and not be afraid;
"For Yah, the Lord, is my strength and song;
He also has become my salvation." (ISAIAH 12:2)

✝ Cast your burden on the Lord,
And He shall sustain you;
He shall never permit the righteous to be moved.
(PSALM 55:22)

✝ The Lord of hosts is with us;
The God of Jacob is our refuge. (PSALM 46:7)

✝ He said to me, "My grace is sufficient for you, for My strength
is made perfect in weakness." Therefore most gladly I will rather
boast in my infirmities, that the power of Christ may rest upon
me. Therefore I take pleasure in infirmities, in reproaches, in
needs, in persecutions, in distresses, for Christ's sake. For when
I am weak, then I am strong. (2 CORINTHIANS 12:9-10)

✝ But the Lord is faithful, who will establish you and guard you
from the evil one. (2 THESSALONIANS 3:3)

✝ I have set the Lord always before me;
Because He is at my right hand I shall not be moved. (PSALM
16:8)

✝ Watch, stand fast in the faith, be brave, be strong.
(1 CORINTHIANS 16:13)

✝   He only is my rock and my salvation;
    He is my defense;
    I shall not be moved. (PSALM 62:6)

✝   I can do all things through Christ who strengthens me.
    (PHILIPPIANS 4:13)

ON HOPE

My heart rejoices in Your salvation
My ululation rises to the high mountain
Bind me with the remedies that lead to life
Keep me under the shadow of Your wings
Fill my belly with milk and honey
Replenish my well with fountains and springs
Grant O Lord that I may be HOPE

✳ ✳ ✳ ✳ ✳

If you are confronted with hopelessness about your personal abilities, you will be strengthened by God's power. If you are not able to, God can. Even if you are not seeking Him, He seeks you as He sought the prodigal son and the lost coin. He stands and knocks at your door to open for Him. How great is this hope that God is seeking you.

SHENOUDA III OF ALEXANDRIA

WORDS OF SPIRITUAL BENEFIT

✳ ✳ ✳

✝ Therefore do not worry about tomorrow, for tomorrow will worry about its own things. Sufficient for the day is its own trouble. (MATTHEW 6:34)

✝ He will not forsake you nor destroy you, nor forget the covenant of your fathers which He swore to them. (DEUTERONOMY 4:31)

✝ In my distress I cried to the Lord,
And He heard me. (PSALM 120:1)

✝ But you shall receive power when the Holy Spirit has come upon you; and you shall be witnesses to Me in Jerusalem, and in all Judea and Samaria, and to the end of the earth. (ACTS 1:8)

✝ Therefore we do not lose heart. Even though our outward man is perishing, yet the inward man is being renewed day by day. (2 CORINTHIANS 4:16)

✝ As for me, I will call upon God,
And the Lord shall save me.
Evening and morning and at noon
I will pray, and cry aloud,
And He shall hear my voice.
He has redeemed my soul in peace from the battle
that was against me.
(PSALM 55:16-18)

✝ Cast your burden on the Lord,
And He shall sustain you;
He shall never permit the righteous to be moved.
(PSALM 55:22)

✝ For I know the thoughts that I think toward you, says the Lord, thoughts of peace and not of evil, to give you a future and a hope. (JEREMIAH 29:11)

✝ Arise, shine;
For your light has come!
And the glory of the Lord is risen upon you.
For behold, the darkness shall cover the earth,
And deep darkness the people;
But the Lord will arise over you,
And His glory will be seen upon you.
(ISAIAH 60:1-2)

✝ Our light affliction, which is but for a moment, is working for us a far more exceeding and eternal weight of glory, while we do not look at the things which are seen, but at the things which are not seen. For the things which are seen are temporary, but the things which are not seen are eternal.
(2 CORINTHIANS 4:17-18)

✝ And my God shall supply all your need according to His riches in glory by Christ Jesus. (PHILIPPIANS 4:19)

✝ Behold what manner of love the Father has bestowed on us, that we should be called children of God! Therefore the world does not know us, because it did not know Him. Beloved, now we are children of God; and it has not yet been revealed what we shall be, but we know that when He is revealed, we shall be like Him, for we shall see Him as He is. And everyone who has this hope in Him purifies himself, just as He is pure. (1 JOHN 3:1-3)

✝ You are my hiding place and my shield;
I hope in Your word.
Depart from me, you evildoers,
For I will keep the commandments of my God!
(PSALM 119:114-115)

✝ With men it is impossible, but not with God; for with God all things are possible. (MARK 10:27)

✝ Let us hold fast the confession of our hope without wavering, for He who promised is faithful. And let us consider one another in order to stir up love and good works. (HEBREWS 10:23-24)

✝ You will keep him in perfect peace,
Whose mind is stayed on You,
Because he trusts in You.
(ISAIAH 26:3)

✝ And whatever we ask we receive from Him, because we keep His commandments and do those things that are pleasing in His sight. (1 JOHN 3:22)

✝ May the God of hope fill you with all joy and peace in believing, that you may abound in hope by the power of the Holy Spirit. (ROMANS 15:13)

✝ Now faith is the substance of things hoped for, the evidence of things not seen. (HEBREWS 11:1)

✝ Therefore we also pray always for you that our God would count you worthy of this calling, and fulfill all the good pleasure of His goodness and the work of faith with power, that the name of our Lord Jesus Christ may be glorified in you, and you in Him, according to the grace of our God and the Lord Jesus Christ. (2 THESSALONIANS 1:11-12)

EPILOGUE

There is not much more to be said that has not already been proclaimed on the previous pages.

I hope that you will always find comfort, understanding, inspiration – and life – through this book.

The journey of attaining Christian virtues is long and winding.

May God bless you with His Holy Spirit and guide your steps through the gift of His grace.

You are always in my prayers.

✳ ✳ ✳ ✳ ✳

ON FAITH

My soul seeks everlasting life
My satisfaction comes from You
Unite me with Your will
Flood me with rivers of living water
Bless my land with summer fruits
Prune my branches of fear and doubt
Grant O Lord that I may be FAITH

ON WORKS

My hands raise in thanksgiving
My reins seek to please You
Shepherd me with Your rod and staff
Ground me in Your will
Anoint my actions with love
Let my light shine that all may see
Grant O Lord that I may be WORKS

ON PRAYER

My groaning resounds eastward
My soul yearns for You
Hear me when I cry
Pull me into Your warm embrace
Let my breath draw us closer
Lift my chin and comfort me
Grant O Lord that I may be PRAYER

ON HUMILITY

My eyes glimpsed my wretchedness
My vessel now emptied for You
Engulf me with Your Spirit
Hold me as the little child
Manage my life as You deem fit
Satisfy my soul as with marrow and fatness
Grant O Lord that I may be HUMILITY

ON REPENTANCE

My tears exceed the sand of the sea
My soul mourns the sins of my past
Wash me with the dew of Your mercy
Restore me to Your salvation
Wipe my eyes with the wool of Gideon
Accept my brokenness as a sacrifice
Grant O Lord that I may be REPENTANCE

ON GRACE

My flesh longs for You
My depths desire Your favor
Decorate me with the wings of the eagle
Fly me to the heights of Your glory
Let my eyes find You
Shower my countenance with Your splendor
Grant O Lord that I may be GRACE

ON FORGIVENESS

My desires chain me to evil
My decisions disappoint You daily
Release me from bitter bondage
Rescue me from the belly of Sheol
Forget my many sins
Raise me from death into life
Grant O Lord that I may be FORGIVENESS

ON SERVICE

My journey seeks the bruised and crushed
My fullness comes from lifting the needy
Help me understand that all are my neighbor
Adorn me with earnest love for all
Season my acts with mercy and grace
Sanctify my ministry of faith
Grant O Lord that I may be SERVICE

ON MERCY
My life deserves eternal condemnation
My soul battles the shackles of iron
Receive me when I cry
Carry me out of my misery
Turn my punishment into salvation
Scent my garments with the fragrance of Lebanon
Grant O Lord that I may be MERCY

ON LOVE
My person pursues praising You
My purpose payment of my debts
Inscribe me on the palms of Your hands
Kiss me with the kisses of Your mouth
Consecrate my heart, soul, and mind
Accept my sacrifice as a sweet aroma
Grant O Lord that I may be LOVE

ON JOY
My heart discovers the paradise of bliss
My hunger satisfied by Your sweetness
Brighten me with the rays of morning
Shelter me from the shadow of darkness
Extend my exaltation to everlasting
Permit my praise to climb the mountaintop
Grant O Lord that I may be JOY

ON PEACE
My anguish drowns my gladness
My resting place forgotten
Receive me in Your midst
Hide me from my enemies
Eliminate my baseless fears
Parade my victorious salvation
Grant O Lord that I may be PEACE

ON LONGSUFFERING
My afflictions sink my head
My sorrow fills fountains with tears
Bring me to a place of rest
Quench me with water not gall
Lighten my heavy burden
Refresh my spirit unto eternity
Grant O Lord that I may be LONGSUFFERING

ON KINDNESS
My arms embrace my sister and brother
My heart knows all deserve affection
Instruct me in the way I should walk
Inspire me with the memory of Your crucifixion
Anchor my thoughts in compassion
Enrobe my actions with hospitality
Grant O Lord that I may be KINDNESS

ON GOODNESS
My tears wash Your feet
My fragrant oil anoints Your head
Regard me in my lowly state
Introduce me to the strength of Your arm
Transform my barrenness to rejoicing
Hearten my labor
Grant O Lord that I may be GOODNESS

ON FAITHFULNESS
My branch has broken from the olive tree
My day of desiccation nears
Graft me in that I might live
Enliven me by the still waters
Remember my place among the green pastures
Ripen my fruits for the harvest
Grant O Lord that I may be FAITHFULNESS

ON GENTLENESS
My feet stamp the sand
My hair bounces with the breeze
Shield me from the coming waves
Secure me upon the cliffs
Grasp my hand
Calm my senses
Grant O Lord that I may be GENTLENESS

ON SELF-CONTROL
My passions burn as a forest fire
My lusts endless as the crashing waves
Force me to hate the devil's delicacies
Satisfy me with bitter herbs
Purify my lips
Curb my desires
Grant O Lord that I may be SELF-CONTROL

ON POVERTY
My sumptuous feast spoils before my eyes
My treasures now the abode of myriad moths
Liberate me of this world's worthlessness
Endow me with keys to Your kingdom
Set my eyes on that which does not fail
Retain my wealth in paradise
Grant O Lord that I may be POVERTY

ON OBEDIENCE
My delight rests in Your commandments
My ears hearken to Your will
Point me toward the narrow gate
Accompany me in bearing my cross
Sprinkle my journey with suffering
Straighten my path that I may find the kingdom
Grant O Lord that I may be OBEDIENCE

ON PURITY

My hands linger in filth
My bed amidst swine
Make me like one of Your hired servants
Give me a ring for my hand and sandals for my feet
Cover my nakedness with a white robe
Crowd my house with music and dancing
Grant O Lord that I may be PURITY

ON WISDOM

My lamp burns as I contemplate Your love
My hope to understand its height and depth
Tell me why I mean so much to You
Send me Your Spirit as my teacher
Remove my thorns of pride and arrogance
Crown my head with the oil of Your grace
Grant O Lord that I may be WISDOM

ON COURAGE

My trembling fills the blackness
My foe listens for my breath
Array me with Your armor
Gird me with Your sword
Magnify my battle cry
Guide my hands to pierce his neck
Grant O Lord that I may be COURAGE

ON STRENGTH

My feet stumble on rocks
My heart fails amidst tribulation
Recover me when I fall
Establish me on Your holy mountain
Elevate my head above my enemies
Fortify my members so I will not be shaken
Grant O Lord that I may be STRENGTH

ON HOPE

My heart rejoices in Your salvation
My ululation rises to the high mountain
Bind me with the remedies that lead to life
Keep me under the shadow of Your wings
Fill my belly with milk and honey
Replenish my well with fountains and springs
Grant O Lord that I may be HOPE

YOUR MEDITATIONS

The following blank pages are included for your personal meditations, prayers, and thoughts.

✳ ✳ ✳ ✳ ✳

Made in the USA
Monee, IL
01 February 2022

89683106R00090